Peel Street

Also by Christopher Nailer and published by Ginninderra Press
Blundstones and a Brown Dog

Christopher Nailer

Peel Street

Acknowledgements

Special thanks to Alan Watts, Stephen Matthews, John Jenkins, Peter Dale and Paul Cliff for comments, suggestions and encouragement.

Peel Street
ISBN 978 1 74027 615 9
Copyright © text Christopher Nailer 2010
Cover design and illustrations by Clare McIver

First published 2010
Reprinted 2015
GINNINDERRA PRESS
PO Box 3461 Port Adelaide SA 5015
www.ginninderrapress.com.au

Contents

Prologue	9
Summer	11
Bill	13
Mitch	15
Belinda	17
Jan	19
Stephen	20
Melina	22
Bruce	24
Carolyn! Ann!	26
Alan	27
Autumn	29
Joe	31
Wilma	32
Theo	33
Kathy	34
Ray	35
John	36
Stan	37
Dennis	38
Janis	39
Winter	41
Vlad	44
Barry	45
Ellen	46
Harry	47
Alexandra	49
Karl	50
Phillip	51
Pam	52

Spring 53
   Derek 57
   Lynda 58
   Franz 59
   Paul 61
   Brinks 62
   Graham 63
   Alice 64
   Doug 66

For Max Serpell, an extraordinary teacher

Prologue

Into January's sunburnt arms
young pilgrims come,
all eyes and ears and voices –
how they grow and grow.
Where are they now?
Not on any sleeping hill.
All somehow touched the blue
maturing core and flared into
the world of full-sized art.
Who held this childish hurt,
that game, burned in
the sea of memory,
idea's time? And what if we
were present once again;
what would be the clue?
A look? A phrase?
An unrepentant forelock?
Or how a smile creeps up in
shyness from the temples?
Perhaps that's how it always is,
how everything you said now
had its essence even then –
a shock of sameness…
To you who thus collided,
bruised and bounced my
bony skin-bag into shape,
played, laughed, ran, rode,
dreamed, punched, stole and
helped to crystallise;

to you these small reminders
of a time before that
last December's parting rush.

Summer brings the morning in the glare and heat;
your bike goes in the front row of the racks now.
Retake your special corner of that dusty ground,
show off on the trestle benches under the peppercorn trees.
First day, before monitors are picked, Mr Appleby rings the bell;
You shuffle into lines. Salute the flag. Sort of march in…

Bill

Bill taught me Australian:
'Air goan?'
'Wot team jabarrik for?'
sharp immediate questions.
Big, burly, red-faced, loud,
he ripped you into his world
like a wash-and-spin-dry,
left you no alternative.
Bill showed me the way to
the fish and chip shop at East Kew –
all the way along High Street,
past Kew Baths, past the dead centre of town –
'Dying to get in, mate!'
And past the Harp of Erin at the top of the hill
with its huge gold harp painted on one green wall –
You could just make it there and back in lunchtime
for a piece of flake and chips wrapped in
newsprint for one-and-six.
And when we went for swimming lessons
in the early mornings,
dry towels twisted rope-thin
round our necks on the way up,
wet, half-furled into headbands
and worn like Arabs on the way back,
he showed us how to survive the
draughty changing sheds open to the sky,
the hard cement and ice-blue tiles,
the compulsory cold plunge shower
before you could dive in:
'Just dunk ya head under!'

Then the rush across the concrete apron
past the 'Strictly No Running' sign and
kasploosh! all nine stone of Bill
dive-bombing anyone too slow.

Mitch

Mitch was a bit of a trickster
with a round head, a quirky smile.
Maybe it was Mitch who showed me the
Mad Old Lady's house on Malmsbury Street,
its front yard full of gnomes and broken china ornaments
and crazy decorations hung on poles.
People said she was a witch;
and if I had to walk past on my own I'd cross over.
'She's crazy but she gives you stuff,' Mitch said.
So one day we took a deep breath and went in;
and she gave us each a cardboard aeroplane.
Mitch lived on Peel Street in one of the timber cottages
just a hundred yards from the school,
past the lolly shop with its spring-loaded
blue wooden fly door with the
worn groove in the top where it
tripped the brass bell
flak! jangle! jangle! jangle!
about a hundred times a day.
And Frank would come out from the back
and sell you a small white-paper bag of
cobbers, bananas, snakes, freckles,
or a packet of sugar cigarettes,
or a Sennett's icy pole for threepence.
I remember one hot day in the holidays
going up to Peel Street to wander in the
silent emptiness of the playground;
I climbed over the low cyclone-wire fence,
walked across the dust-dry yellow powder clay yard
past the two peaceful peppercorn trees where

we'd challenge all comers to a test of balance
on the little kids' trestle benches,
into the solid brick toilet block
to piss way up over the top of the
acrid cement piss-wall, up one, two, three
courses of bricks before the pressure went.
And walking away, down towards High Street,
there he was sitting on his own on the split-edged
veranda planking of the two-window weatherboard house,
feet in the street, looking like he was just waiting for someone
to say, 'Hey, Mitch, let's go and piss up the wall in the toilets!'

Belinda

Belinda was tall and fresh;
she had long brown hair and steady eyes.
Unattainable, her smile already whispered,
'You poor fool.'
Theo cuffed up his shorts and said,
'Hey! Do this. Belinda would like that!'
It made no sense; didn't work for me anyway,
my scrawny shanks no match for his
tanned Greek balusters.
She was the first girl you want to talk to,
find out where she lives, walk her home.
It wasn't far – just along
Peel Street, left onto Malmsbury Street –
this part of town named for
the Old Queen's ministers;
Past the seminary on the left with its thick cypress hedge
and narrow-gauge corrugated-iron fencing –
you could get a good motorbike sound out of it with
the end of a wooden ruler –
to Princess Street – how appropriate –
more or less on my way down to Redmond Street;
Then across and down a few houses
to a grand grey-painted two-storey Victorian place
rented out as flats behind a heavy iron railing;
I saw her go in there one Saturday morning.
But it was no good.
You didn't talk to girls in those days.
The ones you liked were always in a huddle
so it was a bit like taking on four or five at once…
Never even said enough to stutter over.

Tried to draw her once, though –
to take hold of her on paper –
a casual answer difficult when
my mother asked,
'Who's that?'...
Her image stays – a primal memory.
Belinda: the archetype of all my later
dumbstruck admirations.

Jan

Jan had fair skin, an open smile, a white-blond forelock;
arrived from Holland that year, was completely lost.
There was a process for New Australians;
they were allowed to sit at the back. The teachers
asked no questions, set no written work.
They'd point out the arithmetic, smile at the artwork,
wait for the playground to do the migrant English.
And before the first day was out,
the migrant kids'd show they could
pull you off balance on the little kids' trestle benches;
And the world of running, kicking, throwing, catching,
laughing, shouting, scrapping, balancing, swinging,
grazing, picking up, dusting off
soon gave them enough verbs to be going on with;
and in a few weeks the blur of syllables began to clarify.
Some evenings, the Department used our classrooms for
adult English. In the morning, the blackboard would still have
kindergarten sentences:
'John and Betty can run fast.'
We'd sound them out, pretending to be simpletons.
Jan perspired easily;
five minutes into any game and there'd be
beads of perspiration on his upper lip and a
trickle heading down his cheeks out of his sideburns.
But he had sharp eyes and sure hands
and was the best wicket-keeper we ever had.
Crouched forward, frowning fiercely at each delivery:
'Shut up. If I miss the next ball, I'm a bloody Dutchman.'

Stephen

Barracked for the Tigers;
just like one: stocky, short neck,
red face, head down, full of toughness;
a husky voice, urgent, every word shouted;
a bad call by the umpire and he'd be
in there, arms flying, remonstrating hotly.
What was this drive for justice?
Stephen lived on Wills Street in an old
yellow weatherboard house with one of those
brick veranda porches stuck on the front,
about halfway down to my grandfather's place.
Day after day we'd walk the downhill stretch after school,
the old plane trees, full and shady before the SEC'd
lop them back to shanghai stumps to clear the wires;
cicada shells crisp and collectable on the mottled bark.
We'd swing our school bags, kick yonnies along the pavement,
bash any flowers that poked through the picket fences;
it was called 'mucking about'.
His grandma would greet us with crusty Italian bread
slapped thick with butter and honey;
My mother wondered why I always stopped there.
Stephen was good at cricket, Aussie rules,
and one of the fastest runners, and the most untidy –
arms and legs going like a threshing machine,
twenty powerful piston strides to anybody else's;
We were always neck and neck and always
he'd barge over the line just in front;
Always it was Alan first, with style, Dave second,
and Stephen and me sweating it out for third…

The grandma wore all black.
'They never remarry,' my mother said.
I never saw a father round there either.

Melina

Melina was a gypsy, Melina was wild;
she had a big mouth and a loud voice and
far too much to say.
Untidy, wilful, stubborn, rude –
'bold' was the word one teacher used –
Perhaps that was a bad thing?
Today she'd be on Ritalin.
Joe, Melina and I once had to do
a project on modern transport.
I drew the pictures – my masterpiece,
a front-on view of the Southern Aurora
on a curved bit of track, a huge red 'V'
on the nose below the driver's window,
tapering to a long horizontal stripe curving
all the way back along the diminishing line of
silver carriages. She and Joe argued and argued
about what the words should be.
I don't think we ever finished it.
She could be lively, quirky, fun, but most days
there was just way too much Melina.
She was in the violin group; played that loudly too.
Years later, I saw her from the tram on High Street
in her Kew High blazer – cherry red over a
light grey tunic with a thin red thread –
talking to someone outside the Castle Bar,
hair all over the place, arms going like a windmill…
Even through safety glass, across the street,
way too much Melina. Poor thing,

I wrong her terribly. Her only real crime
was I had to dance with her at the school ball.
'Oh yes,' my mother said afterwards.
'I thought your Alice looked very nice.'

Bruce

Bruce was my nemesis.
You see, I thought the way to avoid
being branded a Pommie was to say
I was born in New Zealand.
Then one day someone yelled,
'There's another kid from New Zealand!'
So we either had to fight or become best friends.
And both our fathers were English
and his had flown in the war –
Bruce had a tiny brown photo of him
in the cockpit of an Avro Anson –
and then when you considered his
British Racing Green Royal Enfield bicycle, well…
We cut our fingers and were blood brothers;
carved tikis out of chips of slate and wore them,
a sort of pommie-kiwi brotherhood.
We built the cockpit of a bomber out of
boxes in a dark corner of the garage,
instruments from tin lids nailed to a plank,
flew night missions over Germany by torchlight.
One year we got a job as a delivery boy
for the chemist at the Junction:
Bruce had a bike; I didn't yet.
But I was nearly twelve; he wasn't yet.
I'd pick up the jobs; he rode them around.
That lasted a couple of weeks until
his mother didn't like him getting home so late.
But it paid for an Airfix model of a Junkers JU88
and whatever he spent his half on.
He was short, restless, pushy,

with a round, cheeky face and curly hair;
got it cut really short once; would have
punched anyone who called it a crew cut, though.
In British Bulldog, he'd go
head down, straight into the pack.
And one day without warning, walking home,
he floored a smaller kid from Xavier Prep
right in the street, sat on his chest until he cried.
And sneered, 'Hate Catholics!' as he got off.
He and his parents lived in the back half of a
big old house on Edgecombe Street.
In the workshop his father engineered gadgets
for Vulcan heaters: 'I can't really say what it is
because if it works, I'll make a lot of money.'
We made model boats, planes there;
rambled down by the river;
bent bits of tin into boat shapes
that surely would have drowned us.
And his mother worked too – that was unusual then.
On Sunday evenings after bike bashing
the dirt tracks along the riverbank
we'd sit up with his parents on their big
double bed and watch the *Wide World of Disney*…
We stopped going to each other's places
soon after I went on to Camberwell Grammar.
The last time I went round, his mother said,
'Try and get him to go for the higher-level maths…'
He slumped sullenly on his bed and said,
'She told you to give me a talking-to, I suppose.'

Carolyn! Ann!

Carolyn! Ann! were twins born some years apart;
same pale skin, same orange hair, always
dressed identically. They lived two houses away
on Redmond Street. The dad, a bitter-looking man,
stooped, always in a rush, drove a lumpy old
pale green Vauxhall. Around six o'clock
you'd hear him calling them for tea, 'Carolyn! Ann!'
He ran a newsagents' under one of the arches by
the railway culvert on Flinders Street in town,
hands permanently blue with printer's ink.
When we lived at our grandparents' at No. 19
we mucked around a bit; built a hut out of loose bricks
delivered for a new place going up next door;
sorted through the junk in the council 'Nick-off' truck
when they left it for big stuff the garbos wouldn't take.
For a time, they were useful allies in the war with
Harry's gang – my side of the street all girls;
and now and then they'd get their knees dirty,
skirting the ditch along the cutting behind the
Mental Hospital. From up high above The Boulevard
we'd throw down lumps of clay and watch them
burst on the road below in grenade-like dust bombs.
Later on, Carolyn grew a bit la-di-da... Sat as
far away as she could in class, over by the windows;
went on to Methodist Ladies College, very posh.
Their mother had the same orange hair, fading a bit,
slow eyes, a gentle other-worldly smile when
she opened the front door; spoke a bit oddly;
'Deaf as a post,' my grandmother said.
It was always the dad who called them in.

Alan

Alan had all the grace of a champion
and style to go with it;
tall, dark, he had a friendly, open face,
teeth slightly overlapping.
He was elegant with a cricket bat,
turned and kicked fast and straight in footy;
OK in school work too.
And he was the fastest runner in the school.
Always it was Alan, Dave, and Stephen and me…
He lived with his mother and grandmother
in a small timber cottage painted grey –
the kind with planks grooved to look like
stonework. It had a sunny extra room
out the back and borders of sweet geraniums.
You passed it on the way to the fish shop at East Kew –
Alan rode a fine blue bicycle,
was voted leader of the Biggles club;
We flew patrols in formation around the back streets,
swooping, circling, attacking, dogfighting,
weightless and invincible…
We'd have a milk shake at the Castle Bar,
where Tony with the greased-back hair
chatted up girls from behind the counter,
checking himself out in the etched *Fantasia* mirror
And one day in Sport,
with all the proper batsmen out,
Alan coaxed me through the only innings
I ever lasted past the third ball;
survived Dave's fast bowling that day
with Alan, at the other end shouting,

'It's outside the stumps! Leave it!'
Alan, tall, quiet, generous,
completely without guile.

𝒜𝓊𝓉𝓊𝓂𝓃 settles into piles of russet plane-tree leaves;
it's too cool for swimming; cricket's still OK.
The gang's worked out who's in, who's out, and how
you join the endless wandering of golden afternoons;
you skimp on homework, stay out till the chill comes down…
How many times can you ride the dirt tracks by the river?

Joe

Joe was clever, studious,
already stooped from taking it all in.
He had dark unruly hair, olive skin,
too many teeth; always spoke in a rush,
words tumbling over each other to get out.
His sister Ruth was in my sister's class
a few grades higher.
They lived in another of the big Victorian houses
on Princess Street.
Joe did Cubs with me;
he loved mechanical things.
We got along fine.
I remember his speech about electricity:
when they fired up the first big power station
something went wrong,
'But Thomas Edison took an iron pole and said,
"Put it there!" And it worked!'
a heroic moment vibrant with energy…
Years later, we got off a bus together at university,
talked and talked all the way from Lygon Street
to the main gate, just like yesterday.
But he was doing Medicine; that was serious stuff.
I was into street theatre, Chinese characters,
motorbikes, drinking; we never followed up.
Bet he's a top surgeon or psychiatrist by now.
Bet his parents – Holocaust survivors – wept with pride.

Wilma

Poor Wilma – blowsy, floundering, slow,
defeated already by cares too big for her
downward-sloping shoulders.
She rarely spoke, smiled cow-like,
quietly when the question was beyond her –
shuffled along in a world of her own;
Why wasn't she in Rural School?
She lived in another of the cottages
in the narrow bit of Peel Street between
Frank's lolly shop and High Street, close to Mitch's place –
that row of small timber houses fronting so close that
if a front door or a window was open
you could see right through; a deep emptiness.
I suppose she hung on till fourteen, endured it stoically.
And what then? Married to some no-hoper to
repeat the story? Or did someone care?
Did someone give her life back?

Theo

Theo was the youngest of three Greek gods,
his brothers mighty warriors with cars of their own.
They lived in a big house off Barry Street with a
wide cobbled coach yard.
There were a couple of old sheds, the dad's truck,
two hot Holdens.
The father, small, stocky, grizzled, kept racing pigeons –
this one a beauty, that one cost a lotta money,
that one over there no damn good.
Theo had olive skin, short, dense, black hair,
a small scar in the crown,
the profile of a soon-to-be Achilles.
He liked Belinda; didn't much like Pommies;
thought the American Revolution was a good thing.
I chased him round the school yard swinging out.
Then one day, when they took down one of the sheds,
he fell on a rusty nail and ended up in plaster;
the rumour was he'd broken his leg.
I went round and there he was on crutches.
We watched the pigeons,
purring on their dottle in the boxwood Potala,
rising one entire wall of the rambling old house;
And he showed me the other shed where his brothers
kept their stash of frangers,
put one on to show me.
'You need these when you go out with a girl.
I can get heaps of them, just let me know.'
But then had trouble
getting the floppy yellow rubber thing off.
'Yeah, thanks...' I said, confused...
Just too much secret knowledge.

Kathy

Kathy was mother hen to the Legacy Home kids;
My grandfather did Legacy stuff; I'd heard all about it.
Kathy was short, stocky, a stickybeak, a know-it-all;
she could always see the worst in any situation.
'You'll fall!' she'd call to kids
testing their balance on top of the monkey bars.
And she was a dobber.
She blew the whistle on the planned super
star-fleet battle in Alexandra Gardens – can you believe it?
And when the gang – Franz, Doug, myself –
as initiation, started nicking things from Coles
in High Street – where the home brand was
Embassy with its tiny red Australia mark –
she dobbed on us for that too.
Mr Serpell called the three of us to his desk.
'There's an outfit called the Police who deal with
things like this. I want a list of everything you've taken.
And I'll be speaking to your parents.'
We did our lists – water pistols, a pack of cards,
coloured pencils – more scared of our parents
than of the Police or him;
waited for the explosion to come at the dinner table…
none ever did. And we yelled at Kathy
from as close as we were allowed to go to the girl's
weatherboard shelter sheds, 'You're a dobber!'
But she stuck to her guns. 'Stealing is wrong!'
she flung back at us, round the open doorway.
Maybe she joined the Force herself, had a large family;
would have brought them up superbly.

Ray

Ray fancied himself as an artist,
which was a problem, because so did I.
Every year the Gould League of Bird Lovers
invited entries from the state schools
for the best drawing, painting, pastel sketch
of a native bird. In Art the class became an
aviary on sheets of heavy white paper:
flat-head delinquent kookaburras,
rosellas the colour of tomato sauce,
gothic tawny frogmouths –
only the best went forward.
Most years both his and mine were chosen:
Stalemate.
But one Saturday afternoon –
I can't recall what triggered this –
my father was explaining the arrangement
of the webbing on an army parachute harness –
with a diagram of course;
He knew intimately where it cut you
when the canopy opened with a whack,
and he was a flawless draftsman.
So afterwards I took the sketch.
And next Monday, outside Frank's lolly shop,
in front of witnesses, Ray, looking at
my drawing of the paratrooper, admitted
loud and clear, I was the better artist.

John

John was in Rural School – pronounced
'Rool-skool' – with the deaf and dumb kids.
They had all ages in together.
Today we'd lower the voice a half tone and say,
s p e c i a l – n e e d s.
There were two classes – Rool-skool 1 and
Rool-skool 2. The rest of us were A or B.
But then they changed it to the teacher's initial.
Bruce boasted he was still in Mr Appleby's 6A
and we chanted back, '6S – Success!'
John could sort of hear you but he
spoke with a foggy tongue and
his mouth stretched wide. Two huge pink
hearing aids hung off the sides of his head with
flesh-coloured wires winding down to a
shiny metal box he carried in his breast pocket,
like a cigarette case.
But John was a bit different from the others;
He liked to muck around with us.

Stan

Stan was short, Greek, friendly,
had an easy smile; he was good with a pencil too;
worked out a way of doing the curled brims
of bush hats, pushed back on the head
the way farmers wear them, and paddle-steamers
on the Murray piled up with bales of wool.
I forget his surname and just about everything else:
where he lived, what his family did,
what we talked about. What survives
is an image of him in the playground
one drowsy afternoon, lined up after lunch
half listening to Mr Appleby's announcements
before filing in, up the red cement stairs,
trailing our hands along the cool hard pale green
banister, shiny with the years.
Shadows are falling over where Mr Scrpell
parked his old black Morris Major facing Peel Street;
Stan is smiling with some inside joke,
patchy sun lighting up his golden face.
Just this, and his fingers smudged with pencil,
getting the shading on a picture right.

Dennis

Dennis was one of the Legacy Kids,
from the orphanage in North Kew;
he shared my two-seater wooden desk,
liked cars, invented the ruler-under-the-desk-lid
gear shift. I remember his surname because
he hated it. First names only in state school;
surnames were an insult.
So it was easy to stir him up.
All you had to do was say it and he
would lash out at you, swearing, yelling,
rocking the desk, 'Don't you *ever* call me that!'
Now and then he'd spend the weekend
with his mother in Research.
Said it like it was another country,
with an echo, the way you might say 'prison'.
He'd be back on Monday, sullen, disconnected,
arms hunched over the desk,
fidgeting with the lid. Something about
that surname he really detested.

Janis

Little Janis was small and meek
and had a lazy eye,
her only distinguishing feature
the orange rubber eyeshade suckered onto
the left lens of her blue plastic glasses –
one of those cowl-shaped therapeutic things
designed to prevent forward vision by
the strong eye, screening out the periphery
in case she cheated.
But little Janis was not the cheating type.
She stuck it out.
She was shy, slight, with thin mousey hair.
Her mother dressed her in simple prints,
a bib prefiguring a waitress pinafore.
I can remember nothing she said or did.
She either went completely wild at seventeen
with two strong dark eyes
or married an accountant.

𝒲𝒾𝓃𝓉𝑒𝓇 closes down into vigorous exercise;
rain beats the lead paint off the Library's window frames.
There's an outbreak of footy jumpers and the inter-school sports;
you try out for the relay team; end up in the marching squad.
It's dark now by dinner time; you need a flying helmet on the bike;
bend low over the handlebars racing the cars down Studley Park hill…

Lucy

Lucy was a jolly girl with a big red face;
she bounced through life and made a lot of friends.
Her family ran the fruit shop down on High Street,
next to the delicatessen where a lady with a blue number
tattooed on her wrist worked behind the counter.
Lucy's short, tough, sunburnt father, her mother,
two equally cheerful robust red-faced brothers
all worked in the shop. And in the afternoons and on
Saturday mornings she'd be there, plucking up in her
capable hands pounds of potatoes, carrots, parsnips,
cauliflower, apples, oranges, sometimes onions;
She'd weigh them in the huge hanging scales
in an oval steel dish big enough to take a newborn baby;
then she'd tear a tough brown-paper bag off the wad
held high with string, and in a single gesture, flip it,
blow into it, fill it with the contents of the steel dish
and twist the whole thing twice in the air, leaving
two paper ears to hold, chattering with Mrs High Street –
just now and then, a shout to the brother in mother tongue
for boxes out the back – garlic and broccoli:
sometimes the Greek and Italian customers asked for that.

Vlad

Mr Menzies tried to ban the Communist Party
and then Vlad arrived from Russia
with his sister Katya.
People said they were White Russians,
which was OK.
He also started at the back of the room,
silently coping. We clicked.
In a week or two he was barracking for the Bombers,
broad face beaming.
He was a good sport.
First he couldn't speak English.
Then he could.
Just like that.
Katya had long ripe corn field locks and
the same unusual face;
she was the first blonde I'd ever seen.
Their father cut a dignified portly figure on
Stephenson Street in his tall, black, stove-pipe hat,
flowing beard, black robes and
chain and rosary.
Vlad went on to Kew High up on the hill when
I put my Grammar School blazer on.
And Katya also caught the Cotham Road tram up to
Canterbury Girls'.
'Vladimir is fine,' she said one day our paths crossed.
'He's joined the Kew Harriers.'
'Oh good,' I said, not listening,
her hair all Romanov gold;
Vlad, the good son,
every day less orthodox.

Barry

Barry had no voice box, breathed and
spoke in a wheeze through a neat metal fitting
planted in his throat, held in place
with a small cord round his neck,
like one of those cowboy shoelace neckties.
Barry was in Rool-skool 2 with Mr Cooper –
a corporal in the CMF who coached the
marching squad. And one day Barry said
he was going to have an operation to fix his voice.
He was away for a while. Then he
came back and showed off his new throat.
No metal grid or shoelace tie; just a fresh pink
puckered scar where his thing had been;
was pleased as Punch. Still spoke
in a breathy wheeze but this time
through his nose.

Ellen

Ellen was in the other sixth grade class;
we met each week for violin;
she had long straight fair hair,
a pretty oval face,
serene, graceful.
She practised seriously,
played soaring descant harmonies in
the advanced recorder group too.
And all the silent pheromones said,
'Out of your league, mate.'

Harry

Harry lived on the opposite corner of Redmond Street,
with brothers Andy and Jack, too close for comfort.
Jack, the eldest, was tall, good-looking,
a bit like Cliff Richard; he carried that
grown-up air that goes with a missing father.
My grandmother kept calling them by
their mother's maiden name.
Harry and I got along at first.
At my grandmother's place we made a baby skeleton
out of clay and hid it in a tin box out the back.
Sarah from next door said it was 'rude'.
Well, if no clothes is rude, then I suppose no skin is ruder.
We pretended it was a relative and grieved over it.
And when we finally buried it, it was the oddest feeling.
In the front garden, just back from the street,
beneath the big pittosporums where the milkman left the
wire basket and six bottles of milk,
was a dense clump of hydrangeas we could crawl under
and hide in behind the big spade-shaped leaves.
But Harry and his brothers were already a gang;
they had no need of others. They built billy carts,
raced them in a roar of stainless-steel ball bearings
down the murderous slope at the end of the street.
Harry gave me a rusty old pedal car from their place;
at eight I could barely squeeze into it. I painted it blue and
cranked it along the pavements. It became a *casus belli*;
a raiding party was launched from across the street –
Andy, his mate Bob, Harry – just a bit embarrassed –
came and claimed it back. Our side
held them back for a while with hoses

but in they came. I laid up an ambush for the marauders
under the broad hydrangea bushes as they retreated,
but without the numbers, surprise was not enough.
Some time later, I broke my glasses in the playground;
and with no suitably dramatic explanation, I said
Bob and Andy jumped me in the back lane,
at least, I think it was them…
My sister stormed over and nearly punched their lights out.
Things with Harry and me were never the same after that.

Alexandra

Alexandra
was one of those who
came and went. There she was
in second grade, two rows in front;
and then she left. And reappeared later
in Grade Five, right in the same spot, two
rows in front… Entirely capable, self-contained,
adequately pretty, not in the least unfriendly;
poised perfectly in the middle of
several bell curves; I bet
she made a really good
psychologist.

Karl

Karl reminded us there'd been a war
and who had lost it; loose-limbed, athletic,
taller, older than the rest of us;
ragged waves of thick blond hair and a
rakish chip off one front tooth –
there was something about him…
For a time I was in love with everything German:
Messerschmitts, Panzer tanks, Mercedes racing cars…
Perhaps it was all the war films coming out:
'*Achtung!*' '*Schnell!*' I pumped him for phrases.
His English was good. And he took to Aussie rules,
no problem. Power, speed, raw strength,
turning, weaving, jumping, and all that jostling and
elbowing, scrabbling after the eccentric bounce –
a chance to shove a bit here, settle a score there;
Was good at tunnel ball too, heaving the
leather medicine ball down the colonnade of legs,
grabbing it when he was last man and
belting back to the front…keen to win.
But he was just a bit full of himself,
his voice too loud, just a shade too jovial,
his arms swinging around just a bit too much.
I didn't mind him – his craggy grin,
his earthiness, dirty stories,
manhood just around the corner;
so keen to make a good impression. Perhaps
it was a sudden chill at dinner when I said,
'A German boy came to school today.'
And he never took to cricket.

Phillip

Phillip was The Man. He was It;
wore his hair with the front tumbled forward,
the sides slicked back; sort of
Tommy Johnny Elvis Steele O'Keefe Presley.
Wore jeans before it was allowed
and canvas gym boots with flat rubber soles
and white laces and circular patches
where the ankle bones stick out,
the ones that make you creep along a bit,
head stuck forward in just That Way.
And he'd perfected the half open mouth,
droopy eyelid, slightly stunned look you saw
on all the record covers in Paterson's music shop.
We'd gawk in the window at the new Pye transistors.
Phillip reminded me of the fellow on board *Fairsky*
who sang 'Catch a Falling Star'…
He did good tricks with a Coca-Cola yo-yo;
but he didn't run, play football much, or cricket;
didn't make model aircraft, or ride a bike,
or make up plays or do drawings; or
anything else much. Didn't have to.
He danced with Belinda.

Pam

Pam was the perfect kind of girl –
fair, clear, calm, sensible and, best of all,
she had a sense of humour.
We ended up sharing one of those rattling
wooden two-seater desks,
the kind with two separate solid lift-up bang-down lids;
you could prop them on your forehead,
pretend to be scrabbling for a pencil,
while chatting to your neighbour.
Or you could stick a wooden ruler under the lid and
slide it up and down like a column gearshift –
the kind that new cars had then.
And one cold day, with the bitumen-steeped red gum blocks
the Department bought from the Tramways Board
for school heating glowing in the corner grate,
Mr Serpell asked us to write in a secret ballot
who wanted to pair up in these two-seater chariots –
girls with boys, boys with girls –
'No names, please. Just yes or no.'
And I can remember writing, 'Not perticly,
but I do think the two sexes should get together.'
Must have given him a chuckle –
and she had answered 'Yes',
was the remaining unpaired girl after all the
votes were counted. So I restated my indifference
and for the rest of the year Pam and I sat together.
She did what girls are supposed to do for boys –
settled me down. She was a good mate.
We had a laugh or two.
There was not the slightest frisson.

𝒮𝓅𝓇𝒾𝓃𝑔 pricks up its ears for what comes next…
a haircut at the Continental Barber with the foot-pump chair.
There's a picnic day, running races, the year's winding up,
practice for the school ball and girls you've begun to like.
A list of names goes to the high school opening up on the hill;
you can't wait for break-up and holidays and the long hot summer…

Annie

Annie had a pretty face,
a perky, turned-up nose, cupid's-bow lips;
she wore her dark hair bobbed,
rather like a flapper.
She was competent, businesslike,
had the tidiest pencil case.
It was Annie who pointed out in News
that the year 1961 could be read upside-down.
And she was a good all-rounder.
In my play about General Wolfe's daring attack,
scaling the heights of the St Lawrence in 1759 –
courtesy of *Eagle, the Magazine for Boys* –
she played the French General Montcalm very capably,
ordering a retreat on cue, as Wolfe – myself of course –
victory in sight, expired from a musket-ball to the groin.
Mr Serpell whispered something to Vlad;
his hand shot up:
'Why do you always do stuff about war and that?'
Towards the end of the year,
Mr Serpell did a count of who was going where
to get numbers for Kew High School,
opening next year up on the hill,
and Annie called out crisply,
'Camberwell Girls Grammar School.'
And there she sat neatly on the Cotham Road tram
in her dark navy uniform and straight-set hat
and we occasionally acknowledged, in a look,
our former acquaintance.
Everything was logical.

Everything in Annie world made sense.
I bet she was the best maths/science teacher
her students ever had.

Derek

Derek was a brain box. Twenty years earlier he'd have been
at Bletchley Park; he could work out anything.
He made a catapult gun from the glued-together
cores of industrial tape reels. He invented the folded four-point
paper star ship; if you blew across it the right way, it would spin
on your fingertip, rise into the air, fly a few feet and glide
to earth. We built an armada of them in our desk, planning to
release an invasion on the unsuspecting classroom.
Harry's gang took one apart, realised there was a
double fold of paper at the heart of it, cut this in two,
made twice as many in half the time.
They showed us two bulging desk hangars, throwing down
a challenge. We weren't worried; one of ours could easily
knock out two of theirs. So it was set: Alexandra Gardens, right by the
Town Hall, next Saturday, a battle between the two intergalactic
fleets. Kathy said, 'They'll arrest you for littering.' Then
Mr Serpell got wind of it and made us dump them all in the bin.
Derek was the only kid in school with a hand-knitted
jumper; the colours matched exactly – perhaps the grey
was a touch too light, but the royal blue stripes were right –
what gave it away was the knots didn't have that
smooth machined finish of the ones our mothers bought at the
outfitters, that could stand up to a decent tugging;
his came away, especially at the bottom of the 'V' where
you pulled it on and off. His handwriting was not the best either.
One Monday, when the monitors brought in the big basket
of class lunches, each packed to order in a brown-paper bag,
the mothers on duty had labelled his 'Dowilk'.
We fell about, called him 'Dowilk' for the rest of the week.
He's got to be professor of physics or philosophy by now.

Lynda

Lynda was headed for stardom,
she told us so herself. Year round,
she'd sit just like the rest of us learning
BODMAS and remembering how verbs
are the 'doing words' and guessing the
ending of the day's proverb, carefully written
on the green blackboard in neat yellow chalk:
'Every dog has his…' Bone? Dinner? Walk?
and doing big project cards on the
Snowy Mountains Scheme.
But every October, in the
run-up to a competition, she'd arrive
at school with a huge guitar case
and at the appointed time,
she'd step up as bold as brass onto the
six-inch raised-up platform that said
'Hey, look here, I'm performing…'
and with the instrument on a braided strap
she'd belt out 'You are my sunshine'
with all the front in the world,
swinging her hips and chucking her head
and spicing up the last verse with a
real Connie Francis growl. Then
she'd finish with a sweet smile and a curtsey and a
thank-you to the Banjo Club of Victoria –
and for those few minutes Lynda was
something else.

Franz

Franz was determined to be a bad boy.
Grade One, just three days after Station Pier,
he threw up in class, spent the afternoon
huddled in a wicker chair covered in a blanket,
the closest thing to sick bay,
the stench of state school disinfectant
colouring our nostrils. He was short,
round-headed, awkward, abrasive, unsettled,
proud, always breaking the rules; and he had
the worst rotten teeth you ever saw. He wore
lederhosen to school every day that first year,
said he was Austrian. When we made kites in Craft
I helped him paint a big ostrich on his, 'A national
symbol,' I said... Well, at least it rhymed.
He lived up the far end of Peel Street. His father
was a metalworker, welded in the garage
under a smoked-glass visor, working
thunderous sheets of glistening stainless steel,
copper, tin, with his gas cylinders and more
cutting tools than you'd seen in all your life.
His mother fed us up on fresh-baked cakes.
Franz wasn't much good at sport; which was odd
because he could run like a demon and threw a
wet tennis ball with a real sting to it in Brandy.
His problem was with rules. And he so much wanted 'in'...
But when we were playing Territory – you know,
where you toss a stone and take turns to reach
over your mate's country and cut out the biggest arc
of land you can and add it to your own –
he definitely put his hand down for more balance

to take a bigger slice – everyone saw it –
though he swore blind he hadn't...
And it was not the only incident;
the gang wanted him out.
But then he told a sob story about being in a refugee camp
and bombs going off so we let him back in.
I suppose it was a bit like Russia and Hungary...
His father cut a perfect parabola from pure sheet copper
and gave it to me for the keel of a yacht.
Later, Franz invented The Streak – a superhero with a
grey plastic mac draped from his shoulders –
said it made him run faster;
The Streak stole things from gloveboxes of unlocked cars.
Most curious of all, about Grade Six, the rotten teeth
fell out and the ones that grew down afterwards
were clean and strong and straight and true.
And I reckon in time he grew into them.

Paul

I'd completely forgotten about Paul.
Then years later, my father said,
'I've run into an old school chum of yours.'
It turned out Paul's brother Larry had been
looking after my father's green Morris Mini for years.
They ran the garage on Denmark Street,
collected and rebuilt old Austin 7s.
And when the Mini died one day,
Paul came out to look at it;
'I've been here before,' he said…
At eleven or twelve we'd stood in the farthest corner of
the garden where, on my own small patch,
I'd built a tiny English village out of mud bricks,
with wooden rafters and couch-grass thatch,
roads for cars, a two-storey pub, a humpback bridge;
it even had an airstrip you could land a
Lancaster bomber on –
by the time it was perfectly right,
I'd already grown out of it.
There's Bruce, Paul and me, standing there –
a quick glance back to the laundry windows –
comparing scrotums as the first few
pubic hairs arrived.
'I was more friends with Bruce,' Paul said,
as he lifted the new battery in. 'He's a
squadron leader in the New Zealand Air Force now.'

Brinks

Another Dutch boy, we called him Brinks;
we'd just read *The Silver Skates* in the battered
dark green fraying cloth-bound almost biblical
Victorian Primary Reader for Schools.
Brinks was heavy, had a kind round face, big nose,
not much chin. He liked bikes and yachts;
wanted to be an engineer.
In the lower grades we mucked around together –
would circle the school yard, leaning forward
over imaginary handlebars. Or on windy days
we'd sail across the playground with
handkerchiefs spread like spinnakers.
One afternoon we rode our invisible bicycles,
backs bent, hands forward –
(what on earth are those boys doing?)
all the way down Wills Street to my place after school.
'This is Brinks,' I said to my mother. 'He likes bikes
and yachts and he's going to be an engineer.'
And I bet he was a damn good one.

Graham

Graham had no fingers, just
little buds like when
my mother turned her
kitchen rubber gloves
half inside-out. But
he managed OK, could
pick things up, flip them
around, it was amazing.
And when it was nearly
Guy Fawkes Night and
Mr Appleby did his
Big Warning about
fire crackers we all thought
it must have been that.
Each year we'd make
a huge bonfire at our
grandparents' in a clearing
in the bush block
down the back and send
sparks high into the night sky;
and one year my uncle
set off a jumping jack
right behind my dad;
you should have seen him jump.
And one day Graham said
he was going to the doctor
to see if they could make
his fingers come out.
They never did.

Alice

Ah! Alice, so sweet, so special, her eyes
crinkled; she smiled and melted me;
it was just that there was an extra girl that day
and an extra boy at Madam Wong's
dancing school. 'You, you, together, OK?'
She grabbed us by the arm; she needed pairs
and didn't much care who was aged what.
You see, stocky Madam Wong and her partner,
skinny Miss Lee, were hired each November to
organise a school ball; it was thought to be
good for us. So for what seemed many weeks
we were coached in the polka, the waltz,
the progressive barn dance and – so full of life and
colour – the Mexican hat dance. And I began to
look forward to holding a younger, smaller girl;
Madam Wong up on the stage, shouted out the
steps, belted out the beat on a drum kit while
skinny Miss Lee plonked away on the upright
piano in the corner; and week after week,
Alice would wait for me with her smile, her
long fair hair down her back in one heavy plait,
willing to be led; something that was meant to be.
We never spoke; two years apart, no one did that;
but one afternoon, there, in the distance,
her unmistakable gentleness was walking
little brother Ben home so peacefully…
The big night loomed, final rehearsals at the
new town hall, one of those flat-roofed
60s structures, leaky when it rained.
The last classes floated by in glorious sunlight,

the gardens outside filling with fresh green leaves.
And about the time Kennedy was shot
announcements were made about clothing:
mid-calf frocks for the girls, suits for the boys,
or at least white shirt, dark trousers;
'What about checks?' asked Phillip.
And just before the ball someone got sick;
all the numbers were out and suddenly
Alice was circulating with some dickhead
from Grade Three and I was being piloted
by the undeniable Melina. Oh, Alice!
How can that be?

Doug

Doug was the world's best friend;
red hair, freckles, big nose, splayed teeth;
he spoke slowly as though
his tongue was in the way;
his little brother Jim a miniature of the same.
Doug had the biggest, kindest, most loyal heart,
his friendship non-negotiable.
His father turned chubby chair legs
and other exotic wooden shapes
on a lathe under the house on Denmark Street;
the air rich with pine resin,
the floor a foot deep in shavings.
His parents saved and bought him a bike;
it had bells, a hooter, plastic streamers in
Hawthorn colours on the hand grips;
he was so proud of it.
Doug was Ginger in the Biggles club,
rode with us to shoot down Messerschmitts.
He was a brilliant strategist.
The two of us played battleships for hours
at the silent reading tables in
the library on Walpole Street after school.
And when he'd knocked out all my shore batteries
and sunk all my destroyers, we'd switch to chess
and he'd beat me at that too. The thing is,
Doug's friendship was constant, win or lose.
Someone stole his bike and his father
put together another one from bits,
painted it Hawthorn brown; it had
a fixed gear wheel from a racing bike, was

a monster on the tram tracks but Doug handled it.
And after leaving Peel Street we kept up for a time…
Went to see James Bond *Goldfinger* and other AO films.
Then the family moved to Boronia where they could
afford a house and he wasn't even at Kew High.
And more years later I ran into him again
in High Street: the same red hair, freckles,
big nose, splay-toothed grin. And now
a leather jacket, flying boots, helmet; snap!
We rode two Hondas back to my place in formation;
had a coffee… But the conversation sputtered now
over time and loose connections. I had started uni;
he was thinking about a trade,
the gulf between us suddenly indescribable.

www.ingramcontent.com/pod-product-compliance
Lightning Source LLC
Chambersburg PA
CBHW062157100526
44589CB00014B/1863